influence

a channeled work by The Teachers

influence

the attraction series
book 1

CAROL COLLINS
channel for The Teachers

SP
SYNERGISTIC PUBLISHING

Synergistic Publishing
Alexandria, Virginia

Influence. Book 1 of The Attraction Series.
2023 by Carol Collins

Published by Synergistic Publishing
synergistic-publishing.com

Cover Design: Carol Collins

Channeling sessions for this book were recorded in 4 sessions with a total duration of 3.5 hours. All content was recorded by video and uploaded to a transcription ser- vice. Only grammatical edits were made.

The intent of the author is to provide general informa- tion to individuals who are taking positive steps towards emotional and spiritual well-being. Synergistic Publishing is proud to offer this channeled book.

The Teachers of Jeshua (Spirit)
Influence / [channeled by] Carol Collins.
"Wisdom from Beyond."

ISBN: 979-8-9886421-0-7 (paperback)
ISBN: 979-8-9886421-1-4 (ebook)
First Edition: December 2023

MIND BODY SPIRIT / Psychology

books by The Teachers

Recommended reading order
Ocularity of the Mind (2022)
Mind Body Connection (2022)
Manifestation of the True Self (2022)

The Attraction Series (2023)

The Unfoldment Logbook (2023)

The Essential Material

The Four Pillars of Learning

PILLAR 1: The Foundational Material – the starting point for understanding who your Guide is and why we are having a life. All Pillar One material aligns to and heals the Sacrum Chakra.

PILLAR 2: Idea Reconstruction - otherwise known as law of attraction, deliberate creation, and using the power of thought energy to manifest your life, on purpose. All Pillar Two material aligns to and heals the Throat Chakra.

PILLAR 3: Self-Healing – moving Source Frequency within "The Grid" as a means of clearing unconscious beliefs that stop and/or delay your ability to connect with your Guide team and manifest a life of abundance. All Pillar Three material aligns to and heals the Root Chakra.

PILLAR 4: Intuitive Advancement – verbal and vibrational instruction to open your mind's eye to increase your ability to receive clean, clear. All Pillar Four material aligns to and heals the Crown Chakra.

a pillar 2 book

dedication

For my grandchildren,

May you all find a love of word play, a love of learning, a love for the idea of Life Plan, a zest for life in general, and reliance on your own nonphysical Team.

table of contents

introduction

My dear readers,

I love you so much. I want you to have a life where you choose who to be — who YOU choose to be. Life is. Life will always be choice. I want your choices to be as clean as possible. I want you to have opportunities that are congruent with your Life Plan. I want you to complete and enjoy life. Complete from the perspective of your Higher Self. Enjoyed, based on the perspective of your humanness.

Your world is emotional. Find words, find phrases, find descriptions, find facial expressions, find body language that expresses what you are wanting to receive in return. Boomerang. I like boomerang to describe this. What you send out, you receive. Therein lies the definition of law of attraction. Boomer-ang. What you send out, you receive.

This book is not hither and yon. It is straightforward, encapsulated, and full of learning without fluff. I teach verbal therapy. There will be more like this book and perhaps activities, journals, and games identified so that you can learn, plus integrate. Both are necessary. I guide you. I shield you. I teach you. I provide sustenance for the inner mind. It is the one that throws the boomerang. It is also the one that catches the boomerang. It is law of attraction, person by person.

It is part of this life experience. I want you to be able to use it. See it as an ability and you will be able to capitalize on it. Words matter, thoughts matter. They direct your life. I and others like me guide you along the path because most of you have no awareness about this inner attractor.

Phraseology. I like that term. I like it even better when you choose phraseology that is underscored with happy. You are the creator of your own life; others may influence you, others may attempt to influence you, but you are capable of choice. Choose by way of your guidance system, the emotional kind.

Learn first, then teach. Learn first, integrate, then teach. I am with you as you read this book. If you feel sensations in your body, look up and to the right as a simple acknowledgement that I am present. If you do not feel a tingle sensation, then your mind is simply not ready to produce that action to you. Read the book again and you will. It is a small book and it might take two full readings to feel a physical sensation for some. Worry not about it; it is where your inner mind is on the learning of how to show you physically the presence of myself.

Acknowledging the physical sensations while you read is also an acknowledgment of my presence. When you, the physical human being, acknowledges my presence, the interior part of you that throws the boomerang learns that you are wanting Source Knowledge, nonphysical guidance, and it is good that you do.

We guide you, not emotionlessly, but we combine perfect position with perfect timing with perfect knowledge and we subtract nothing. For we know what you are able to accomplish. We show you what the path can be. How do you get there? Implementing verbal therapy.

Be at peace as you read this. It is a playful, inquisitive, yet meaningful Wisdom book. Carry it with you. Write in the margins. Dogear the pages. Treat it like a manual.

I like books that are healthy for your mind. This is number one in the companion set. Where you lead, I follow. Where I lead, you do not. I teach you that it is good for you to do so. Life gets better, relationships get better, synchronicities abound. Joy, happiness, and love entwine with life experience. I want that for each and every one of you. You get what you think about, and I think about that, always with you in mind.

Forever yours,
One among The Teachers

influence

chapter one

This book is all about thoughts. What is a thought? A thought is a concept. A thought is a coming together of different vibratory elements to form an interior question or statement. An interior question or statement simply means that, somewhere, the interior part of you has decided on something. The interior part of you. Let's talk about that first.

You have this physical form, and you know what you look like. You have eyes and ears and nose and mouth and teeth. When you smile, you recognize your smile. When you look in the mirror, you recognize who you are. You hear your voice, you know that it is you; you also know when you are speaking.

The mind registers certain things automatically – so automatic that you don't even recognize the momentary nugget that is taken in. "I breathe easy, I breathe raspy, I smell something pleasant, There's an aroma that's awful, The music is delightful, What is that screeching, It's a beautiful day outside, Ugh, the weather is terrible, I'm not going anywhere today."

The inner mind absorbs data and transforms it into categorized bits of information that eventually equals a decision, an opinion, a preference. These become your likes and your dislikes.

I am teaching you that your thoughts don't have to mean anything so that you can discover what you prefer. You already have a preference – you simply do not know what is. You think you have a preference, but you do not know why that preference is yours. Remove the influence, find your true preference.

I say, you simply don't know who you are.

You have influence thrust upon you from the very moment that you have awareness within. Awareness of your physical environment. Awareness that others speak. Awareness of sounds, of taste, of smells, of tactile sensations, and the opinions of others.

There is no telling what this world would be like had you not been able to express, in one way or another, your own personal opinions. This world being what it is, and everyone having the ability to express their own opinion, people no longer know what their own opinion really is.

Why do you like soft? Why do you like math? Why do you dislike the color blue? Why do you feel bad when it rains outside? Why do you like galoshes? Why do you...?

I know why you do.

You believe that you have no control over what you receive in life, or what you think about, or who you are. You are the one who *does* have control. It is all up to you and that is the whole answer. It's not a satisfying answer because it does not give you enough to learn from.

I will come back to that point again and again in this book. Thoughts create, and those thoughts do not have to be your own.

When an infant lays on the carpet, a very soft carpet, it feels carpet. It feels, and that is all. It does not know soft from rough. It just knows carpet. If the child is lying on the linoleum floor, the child knows that he feels, and that is all. The child does not know the plastic touch of linoleum -- smooth, in some cases, a little rough in others, those minute bumps you feel when you touch it with your fingertips or the groove of the design. An infant has no data. None.

It does not register where it is as the floor. It does not register where it is as carpet versus linoleum. You teach your child down versus up because you pick a child up and you lay it down. It begins to associate. Down feels like this, up feels like this. Being spoken to feels like this. The words do not register as anything initially.

The mind is a very quick learner, how-ever. The vibrational tone of objects is indiscrete to an infant, as well as to you. You do not feel a physical pulse emanating from rugs or chairs, or a lamp post or even a human being. You just know what those objects are. You know if those objects have a beating heart and sometimes you don't care and that's when you squash a bug.

I want you to care about data and forget about preference altogether. You think you like sunshine. Why? You think you like warm. Why? You think you like snow. Why? You think you like expensive furniture. Why? You think you like glasses without spots. Why? You think you like clean sheets or clean socks or a clean face or clean hands.

Why? All of you have an answer.

Because I don't like dirty hands. Why? Because I was taught to wash my hands. Why? Because they were dirty. Why were you taught to wash dirty hands? So I wouldn't put them in my mouth. Why? Because of germs.

Okay, so now we get to a different answer. Now the question simply remains: What is a germ? You don't have a direct answer.

It is a molecule? It is a virus? It is plant material? Literal dirt? You are told it is not to be ingested, just like grease and motor oil. Who decided that motor oil was bad for you? Someone that saw what ingesting motor oil did to the body or the ingredients of it. But how did the body become disagreeable to those ingredients?

Which came first, the chicken or the egg?

I am not going to put your human earth-born knowledge ahead of Ours. But I am going to intrigue you and, hopefully, inspire you, and entertain you a little bit. But mostly, I am going to educate you. This is an important subject and I like this subject very much.

Thoughts create.

When you think, "I like meaningful conversations," the human being registers "I" and "me" and "like." The human being registers preference as a yes, as acceptability. Simply because you understand language, you teach yourself more and more what it is that you think you prefer. "Oh, I love this, Oh, I like this, I can't stand that, That's gross, Ewww, no don't do that, Don't put that there, That's not good for you, Why did you...?"

Language – the root of all evil. Playfully, I say that. Language is, however, the root of communicating. Language can be precise or extremely imprecise, but your human physical mind cannot tell the difference.

You might add a smile or an emoji nowadays, or you might shake hands and slap each other on the shoulder to add some levity. But you do not know whether someone added that gesture to cover up their vulnerability or if it was levity inherent in the comment. You don't know. Even if you were to ask and the person answers, you do not *know-know* if what they tell you is true.

Now, I don't encourage you to disbelieve everybody and everything. But this is an interesting topic because you *don't know*. When you think about it that way, you simply agree rather than argue. "I do know, I know exactly what he meant" turns into "You're right, I truly do not know." Isn't that interesting?

What you do not understand is that you do not know why you prefer the things that you prefer. Why you don't do the things that you want to do. Why, when you do the things that you don't want to do, you feel bad. Some of you feel bad, some of you feel shame, some of you feel guilt, some of you feel downright obnoxious, coercive, bold, proud of yourself, or sneaky.

Just adding those words gives you something to play with. I teach you not only how to narrow down what you prefer, but how to use language to express yourself.

Not for any other reason than *you can.*

How many of you use the word "sneaky" as an adult? How do you use it? With eyes looking down full of shame, as in, "I was sneaky," or with a thread of delight, as in "I was sneaky about it"? Is it okay to be sneaky? That's another question.

I say of course it's okay to be sneaky whether you feel good about it or not. It's okay because in this world you get to choose. That's what being a person is all about. There are no rules such as, "Thou shalt not because we said so." That rule is inaccurate and does not exist from our Knowing.

So many of you believe things – thou shalt not, thou shalt not, thou shalt not.

This book is my favorite topic because it allows me to teach you something about yourself.

Who are you? Each one of you is a different person and so each answer is different. Who are you? What do you know about yourself? I say, nothing. You don't know anything about yourself.

From the moment that you were admonished for the first time, you began receiving influence. What was the first time? All of you will have a different answer.

"I don't remember, Most likely when the doctor spanked me, when I touched something hot, or I never got in trouble."

So many different answers. The moment that you began this life, you began to receive admonishment, because it comes from people.

People admonish in a compliment. "You look pretty." In the saying of those words, the opposite is always also said. You cannot look pretty any more than you can look unpretty. You cannot be pretty, nor can you be ugly. But words tell you that you can.

Words tell you that you are or have been or will be. Thoughts create. When you hear them, your mind has learned something. When you repeat them, your mind learns it again. When you repeat them to another person, the other person learns it for the first time or again. And on it goes.

It might seem trivial to some of you. Pretty is, as the saying goes, in the eye of the beholder. Okay. I go deeper than that. What is pretty? Why is pretty, pretty? Let's go even deeper, who cares?

We don't. We don't want you to.

When you no longer feel pretty or unpretty then you are you in that moment in time. When you are you in that moment in time, without the weight and heaviness of the influence of others, you free yourself from the opinions that you have been taught.

Even though this is truth, there is also the knowing that you cannot escape it. If you decided to become a monk and live in solitude, you would still know language. You might not hear the influence of others, but you would still look about your location and you would know comfort, discomfort, satisfied, dissatisfied, needing more, wanting more, rough, pleasing, unpleasing, barren, thirsty, hungry, the caterpillar will turn into a moth or a butterfly, the withering tree will die, fire is hot, I am peaceful, my home is unlike others, my life is different...

From there, you simply add on. My life is different in a good way. I'm satisfied with my life. But are you? You truly do not know, but it is an interesting subject, nonetheless.

How can you use this? It is awareness.

When you are aware, not only of your surroundings but who you are within your surroundings, the thoughts and the opinions and the influence of others rests on you differently. The opinions of others become less revealing to you. The opinions of others matter not. Truthfully, they matter not as much.

When you start to investigate your own language skills, then you have the opportunity to choose different verbs, adjectives, and phrases, as well as, quite frankly, whether to say something out loud or not. You are an influencer. What you say influences others. What you drive influences others. The clothes you wear influences others. The way you wear your hair influences others. The shade of lip gloss influences others. The style of your dress shoes influences others. Choosing a Windsor knot or a bowtie influences others. The way you physically present yourself to the world influences others, as well as yourself.

You are one of the others to everybody else on the planet – directly and indirectly. When you meet someone, that is direct. When you watch a television show or a commercial, that's indirect. The underlying reason you do what you do and like what you like and don't like what you don't like and say what you mean or not is because of influence from language.

An interesting experiment is to simply remove one word from your vocabulary. Choose a word, any word. How about, yes. No longer say yes and replace it with okie dokie. What happens? You feel strange. You might feel awkward. You might feel empowered. You might feel silly. It might feel unnecessary. It might feel of no value. It might cause shame, depending on who you are saying okie dokie to. How many formal documents would you feel comfortable substituting inserting okie dokie for yes? Check no or okie dokie.

You would not do it in all cases because it is not accepted to be able to choose your own words. That is why you have legalese, so that you do not choose your own phrases, because your own phrases might get you in trouble.

Now, there's a lot that I could pick apart in that statement alone.

The example is simple yet profound. Why can you not say okie dokie in a formal document? I'll answer for you. It's because someone told you that you are not allowed to, and they told someone, and they told someone, and they told someone, and they told someone until it became wrong. Not just not allowed – wrong.

Make no mistake, it is the wrong word choice.

You know where I'm going now – "wrong word" choice. You know what that means. All of you have heard, "That's the wrong word, you stated that incorrectly. The proper phrase is…" You've heard it thousands of times, so your mind knows that there is a right and a wrong. Not just a right and wrong way to say something, but that there is right from wrong.

When you say, "You look pretty today," the mind ingests, *I look pretty, and I did not look pretty on a different day.*

That is why you react and respond in the ways that you do, either to that individual statement or in general, so that you do or do not receive more of that type of statement. Then you see where the influence goes – trends, tracking, methodology, prescription drugs, cosmetic surgery, skinny jeans, baggy pants, culottes, gauchos, suspenders, overalls, feather in a cap, outdated fashion, wrong place and time.

You teach simply by being awake and you are taught simply by being awake.

Look out any window and observe what you see. In this moment in time on this day, February 26, 2021, at exactly 9:30 a.m. on the East Coast of the United States here in Cranberry Township, Pennsylvania, at the house at 115 Meeder Lane, looking out the double window of this makeshift video room where we are recording this book.

At this moment, there are three men visible. One pulling a cord, one hammering, one out of view currently and now back in view, walking. The walking one has a toolbelt with things dangling, orange gloves, white hard hat, navy blue or black jacket and blue jeans, steel-toed shoes. There is a whirring, the sound of a motorized saw and a click, click, click, click – the sound of a nail gun. One is gesturing with the right hand, and another comes into view. An elderly, very mobile, thin man is the only one wearing sunglasses. He has a long gray beard down to his chest.

What are they doing? They are building a home; they are constructing something. The eyes quickly take in another human being way off in the corner, who has darted in and darted out. There's a water retention pond, two-fourths of it covered with plant life. The snow has receded, melted, and mud and soft earth remains. The sky is hazy, yet light blue with soft white clouds interspersed.

Way over on the hillside stands a home not fully constructed, not yet under roof but nearing so. It is large. There is a man running towards it, a measuring tape stretched out. He registers the numbers and now they are being written down. Boards are being lifted and piled, removed from one area, piled to another area. Purposeful activities.

They are working. They are making. They are measuring. They are moving. They are running or walking. They are standing. They have a temporary safety fence made out of wood around the perimeter because they are on the second floor.

Here's where it gets interesting. The ply-wood has been laid down on the two-by-fours that framed out the ceiling. These men, with no harness or safety net, while there were no precautions in place, simply walked across the top of these boards to get from point A to point B.

Now that they are using power tools and moving about in a quicker fashion; there is a perimeter installed to ensure that no one falls off the structure. If that philosophy was in place the whole time, they could not have constructed the ceiling.

How can you construct something if you aren't allowed to get up there to do it? If you can't be up there without a safety perimeter, then you can't be up there. But you can't construct the safety perimeter unless you're there before one is put up. So, you can never get there.

Someone decided when the proper safety precautions needed to be in place and when they didn't.

How did they do that? Research says... Studies show...

What do the men feel? They are in this moment having many thoughts, some known, some unknown to them. Cold. Overworked. Tired. Hungry. Talkative. Focused. Humorous. Steady on my feet.

Safe. Proud. Eager. Bored. Dissatisfied. Happy. Strong. Weak. Willing. Aggravated. Out of breath. Curious. Stamp of approval. Recognition achieved. Satisfaction thwarted. Denied access. Perimeter complete. Onto the next phase. Safety standards enacted. Job well done. Get it right the first time. Join our crew. Get a pay raise. Be proud of what you make. Doggone it, I messed up (insert f-u-c-k because that is the word these particular men would use). Let me show you something. Explain this to me. Where does this go. Lowering standards. I would not do it that way. Because the boss said to. Where is the gosh-darn drawing, oh wait, that's right, page two. I need coffee. I'm hungry.

It is now 9:41 a.m. So in those eleven minutes, we captured but a fraction of what the human being can take in. The eyes of Carol alone saw thousands of influencers in those eleven minutes. Every one of them taught something. Every one of them created something – something more, something less, something new.

Change is not inevitable. Change is constant.

Even though these men are still doing what they were doing, they're doing it in a different place on this ceiling/floor. They have different thoughts, different movement, different motions, different conversation, different activity, many different things to respond to, to register, to talk about, to think about, to have a reaction to.

On it goes and on it goes.

This single workday changes these men. They are not the same men when they go home that they were when they left home, wherever home may be. The home is not the same, nor are the people or the plants or the animals or the objects within the home, because nothing remains stationary.

It appears to, I know. Nevertheless, the opinions that these men have, have changed. They've either grown stronger, altered, or become less but they never remain the same. Over time, the change becomes evident or becomes resident knowledge.

So how do you do something different? You start paying attention to what you are paying attention to and then begin to ask yourself some questions.

What else is there to look at? Start noticing different things and then you have something to really have fun with. You start to ask, "Why did I not notice that the first time?"

Life is interesting, no matter which way you look at it. Life is interesting when you decide that you want it to be. Until then, it's another day that you look pretty or unpretty – although, from our perspective you are exactly where you are and who you are, and we delight in every moment of your life.

This book is going to teach you some things about how to look at your life in a way that allows you to be uninfluenceable. Then you will begin to understand that some of the things that you think you enjoy, you don't. Someone else created that thought in you. That is influence.

When you start to recognize that you do have preferences and when you start to become free enough to explore what your preferences are, you free yourself from the binds that others tied to you. Then you get to be who you really are. You then create, and create, and create, make, and make, and make, do, and do, and do think, and think, and think, say, and say, and say, because then, you are who you really are. Or, as much as you can be in any point in time.

Influence comes every which way. Your awareness to your surroundings is step one.

When people simply understand that words don't mean anything, they relax, life gets a little easier. It's not the easiest thing to put into practice. It's one of those things that you can understand where we're trying to go with it, but seems impractical, impossible to implement. You can know it's true but throw your hands up because you are surrounded by influence. I know you are. The idea is to understand words are just words, but the emotional attachment to them is something you alter. If you throw your hands up and say, "Well, it's just the way the world is," then for you, that's the way the world will continue to be.

Don't not try just because it's daunting, because it *is* life-changing. Disillusionment goes away. Anger goes away. Fear goes away. I won't even say that you will be left with dissatisfaction, because it doesn't have to be that way. You don't have to live like a monk and meditate for hours on end to reach happiness.

You simply need to recognize that words do not hurt. Your attachment to the emotions that are triggered by words, well, that's a different story. Minor detail? No, because one influences the other. I start with influence.

Everything influences everything, but I don't say that there's only one influence. Every action has a counter action. Again, that's not what I'm saying at all. What I am saying is that every action teaches something. What it teaches is dependent on who it is being taught to, including yourself.

When you speak out loud, you're teaching something to yourself about what you think. If you are saying some-

thing, someone else learns directly or
indirectly. They might overhear you or
they might see the scowl on your face,
or the smile. You are always teaching
someone else in every case.

What are you teaching? It is always
that disillusionment, anger, love, fear,
disappointment, happiness, joyfulness,
and glee exist.

I do want you to recognize that happy
is a better emotional cord than
disillusionment. Before we get there, I
want you to not underestimate the
powerfulness of what I'm saying.

Words are letters strung together. That
fact can resonate with you on a very
deep level if you allow it to. A word is

just a word. Any word that causes you to feel anger, you have associated anger with the word. In other words, you have a belief about that word or a belief about how that word was used. That's you, not the word.

You have power over you what you do. You have power over what you think. If you slow down long enough to evaluate your emotions and what the triggers are, then you can start narrowing down words to eliminate from your vocabulary if you are the one saying them, or, change your decision about the word if you are not.

Why do I say decision? Because you have an emotional cord to words, a conscious or unconscious commitment to that decision matters not.

If a parent teaches you the "N word," you learn what that word is and that it is okay to use – so you might. At the same time, the world teaches you that it is not okay to use it. Now you've learned two things. Which do you choose?

Does the situation matter?

Let's use a different example. How about the "F word," you know which one. Four letters strung together that can mean so many different things. Why do you say it? In what context do you normally use it? Are you afraid to use it in front of certain people? Do you abstain from saying it? Do you have no awareness of how often you say it? How do you feel when you say it, brave, casual, angry, passionate, lonely, or disappointed?

When you find the emotional cord, then you understand what your decision about that word is. "I use that word when I'm around certain people" is how many of you may put it when the situation warrants the use of the F word.

Okay, what situation is that? Out at a bar drinking, everybody's laughing, and it just slips out left and right? When you're angry, and pound your fist on the table? Which is it for you?

The connotation of the word is exactly what I am talking about. What is the connotation of the word to you? Or what are they, because one simple word doesn't have one simple connotation, one emotional chord. There are reasons why you choose the words that you do. When the word comes out of your mouth, do you immediately want to take it back because you feel shame, or does it not even register in your ears?

Only you choose to say or not say any particular word or phrase. We're not just using the F word or the N word to point out bad words. We're saying good versus bad, happy versus sad, day versus night, black versus pink, blue versus green, old camouflage versus new camouflage, Nike versus Adidas, Wal-Mart versus Target. Why do you say the things that you do? Do you say it snarky, funny, judging, critical, or silly?

There's always some kind of emotional cord with everything that you say, truly there is. I point out that emotion shifts because of what you said or how you said it. You can hear someone making fun of a person. The Inner Being within shies away from making fun of people, but outwardly you might accept what others are saying so much that you join in. Or, you agree with them, which is also joining in, albeit quietly.

There is a way to evaluate what the cords are that you hold onto to reveal who you are. As an example, Susie walks into school one day, Johnny looks at her and says, "What are you doing here? I thought you had detention." But he says it with the tone of, "You got in trouble." He says it loud enough for others to hear. The tone is not one of concern.

Now read that first sentence two or three times. How do you read it, given the information? What emotional situation are you conjuring? Confrontation? Absentmindedness? Casual concern? Idle conversation? Awkward flirtatiousness? Believe it or not, those are only but a few. What are the situations that come up for you?

Those, dear ones, are the moments from your life, from the lives of others around you, or what you have an awareness of.

chapter two

Johnny says to Susie, *What did you do, anyway?* Susie answers, *I don't know.*

How did you read that? How would you finish the sentence or the conversation? Pause here a moment. What are the scenarios that could take place from that prompt?

That you have no control over what you think about is false. You are the only one that has control.

If you are sitting at a table with others and someone says something, you cannot unhear it. This is true. And you might believe there is nothing you can do except be silent and listen. However, you can shift your awareness to something else and ignore the rest of the conversation, or you can ask for clarification or offer an alternate opinion. You can storm out, you can quietly leave the table. You can make a phone call and step away from the conversation altogether. You can confront the person, and then the string of what follows becomes another potential list.

Why is this valuable? Because it is how you have been influenced. You cannot think of an example that is not resident in your mind. The things that are resident in your mind is everything you have ever been exposed to. The things that come to mind quickly and easily are those things that you have been exposed to, frequently or recently.

You have no real opinion. You have been influenced from the moment you are born. Does that make this book invaluable, useless, or theoretical only? No. Awareness is powerful because it is the necessary first step towards change.

You have the power of Source at your fingertips. What does that sentence reveal to you? What emotions rise to the surface when you read it? If you close the book, open it back up in two days' time and reread the same sentence. Do you have the same emotional response? Some of you will. Some of you will not because in the reading of this book, some of you will feel a shift in one direction or the other. That shift can be towards happiness or away from it.

What are your trigger words, your hot buttons, your go-to words? Do you use them? When? Why? With whom? How do you know they are trigger words? What response do you receive that tell you that you have hit someone else's hot button? Emotional reactions are a clue, but not the answer. Someone may respond with a shrug of the shoulders. Internally, they might be seething and biding their time. How do you know whether you have impacted them or not at all? I say you have impacted them, period. You have because everything that you are exposed to has an impact. It might not register in your aware, conscious mind, but it does not need to be resident in that awake, aware state to have made an impact.

It is how beliefs are born. Quiet influence over time creates a belief. That belief causes you to respond emotionally as well as with behavioral tactics to receive more or less of that influence, depending on your current focus. When you begin to investigate some of these things, it can get quite interesting.

How did I find my way to the belief that I am forgetful, as an example. Where did that belief come from? Do I believe it? Am I just occasionally preoccupied or have I truly become forgetful?

What does having a belief mean? A belief within means, quite simply, that there is a small dictator within, and that dictator decides what you believe in.

The voice of the dictator is so soft, you don't hear it. When you avoid making your bed, why? When you repeatedly wash your hands throughout the day, why? When you freeze up when someone asks you to stand and recite a poem, why? If someone asks for your name and you give them your first name only, why? When you speed through a yellow light, why? When you forget to pick up your dry cleaning, why? The dictator within has registered enough of these thoughts to have decided what you get to experience.

There are beliefs and then there are underlying reasons for those beliefs, and the dictator within always pleases the beliefs. That is how you end up with the life that you have. Beliefs are born because you've been influenced your entire life.

So many of you will say, "I don't have anger, I'm a happy person." Yet you just can't get that promotion, or you just can't manage to get everything in one trip to the grocery store. Why? Are they tied? We know they are. You are not able to decipher all of the whys and why nots.

Suffice it to say this is an interesting topic, is it not? Why do you have the personality that you have? You were not born with a personality. Your personality is your beliefs playing themselves out all day long, every single day.

Another question that you can ask yourself is, what do you not enjoy about your life? I don't enjoy that I only have a handful of friends. Okay, let's play with this one.

Did you always have only a handful of friends? The answer could be yes or no. Did you live on a farm and not live near people? Let's presume the answer is yes. Did you go to a school where the kids who lived in the country were made fun of? Let's presume not. Were you the eldest? Let's presume no. Were you the middle child? Let's presume no. Were you the second to the youngest? Let's presume yes. Was someone in your family deaf? Let's presume yes. Let's stop there.

Perhaps there was just less speaking out loud in your particular home, and so you learned to be shy because you had not practiced speaking in front of others frequently. There's no good or bad in that. It's just tying a current manifested way of thinking to your own life's circumstances.

You think, therefore, you are. Truth.

But what you think is not you. What you think is the culmination of influences that have been thrust upon you. Because of that you are the culmination of moments that have no true bearing on who you are. You are a product of your environment. That statement is false. You are a product of your own thoughts about the influenced experiences of your life. Life equals influencer. You are a product not of your environment, you are a product of your life. You can change it, reverse it, amplify it.

There are things to delight in and there are things to undo. Do not get critical toward yourself when doing these exercises. Simply look at them as information. Hold no emotional cord, though thoughts and feelings will rise to the surface. Look at those thoughts with ambivalence. They have no weight, they have no bearing, they have no influence if you do not allow them to. Awareness is key. Recalling the awareness that you are receiving from reading this book. That's key number two: learning in the moment is what is happening.

Some of you will close the book and believe it was a good read and that you have satisfied your curiosity about a dictated book. Some of you will read it from cover to cover, find no value in it, and remark that it sounds like every other self-help book. That's okay. We do support these types of teachings wherever they come from. Others of you will read it two or three times, cover to cover, underlining, dog earing, writing in the margins, and taking notes. Some of you will put it to practice. Some of you will recommend it to others. Some of you will hold it close to you and say, "This book changed my life. I'll buy you one, but I can't give you my copy. It's too precious."

Hold no emotional cord to anything, even the words that I write to you. Learn from them but hold no emotional cord, because when you do that dictator within takes note of it and adds to a belief or creates a new one. I want you to exit this life with fewer beliefs than you began with. And yes, you do begin life with a few beliefs. It is one reason why the world is what it is.

The world has some beliefs that are resident in it. Those are the beliefs that you start with and then you simply accumulate life experience – and then all hell breaks loose (smiling). Or you come upon articles, magazines, books, videos that help undue the influence. There are many. This is but one, and it is mine and this is how it came about.

On March 20, 2019, this woman, Carol sat in her red chair as she did every day and began to shut the world out as she listened to the sound of a clock ticking. It was just enough for me to silently teach the inner mind to be quieted. There was a conversation I had with her inner mind; she heard it not. It went something like this:

"Breathe in, breathe out, breathe in, breathe out, breathe in, breathe out. We are who we say we are and we are wanting you to be happy. We are wanting you to know that life is meant to be good. We love you so much. Life is meant to be good, and we love you so much. Breathe in, breathe out, breath in, breathe out. Life is just a moment in time. As such, it cannot hurt you, it cannot hold you captive. Release your fear, release your entanglement with fear. Breathe in,

breathe out, breathe in, breathe out. You have our undivided attention."

Those words came from me. Carol's mind was soothed and became quieted the more she sat in these silent meditation sessions.

Quieting the mind is necessary to soothe the emotional cords that you have to life experiences. When the emotional cords are soothed, you feel them less. When the cords soften you feel happy easier. When you remain in that position day after day, something new happens. Your emotional guidance system resets itself. It adjusts to the new frequency that flows through you. Anger, shame, embarrassment all have different frequencies. If those are the predominant emotion that you are feeling day after day, then your body gets used to it. When you soften the emotional cords that you have to life, the density of your personal vibrational countenance must shift continuously upward. Disillusionment turns to disappointment then eventually turns to freedom.

After many months of these silent conversations with me by way of meditation, something started to happen. The emotional cords softened to a degree that we could speak freely. Not to her, but to her mind. Her body began to adjust to our frequency. It happened swiftly. Although at first, she barely noticed it.

When she did notice it, she loved it, and it grew. What grew? Motion. Movement. Mobility. Softly flowing movement of the face. Soft circles, soft swaying, soft lifting up, soft receiving. Softly, softly, softly the body began to acclimate to us. The months went by and the movement did not go unnoticed. She began to say one sentence to herself, "Is this my body acclimating to Source Energy or is it communication I am not yet translating?

She repeated that phrase to herself day after day for approximately two months. Then, on that day, March 20, 2019, during this quiet conversation which was later in the day than usual but true to her daily regiment, nonetheless, her face simply turned to the left, slid to the right, turned to the left, slid to the right, turned to the left, slid to the right and then turned to the left once again.

Then something fun happened. The interior mind woke up and understood that I was speaking to it. It knew Source Frequency was flowing consistently but, in that moment, the interior mind recognized something new. Within the frequency were the words Infinite Intelligence. The mind, believing that I was speaking to it, simply made a motion with the face of the infinity sign. In that moment, Carol heard the word "infinity." It registered in her mind as the motion was manifesting.

Then the motion stopped. She sat a moment, and the movement began again. She recognized that the motion her face was making was the symbol you know of as infinity. When she acknowledged the symbol, the motion stopped again. In that way, I was able to tell her mind, as well as her, "I are here and I am ready to have a conversation with you."

The human being glowed with happiness. The statement for the mantra that she had been saying, "Is this my body acclimating to Source Energy or communication that I am not yet translating?" revealed itself as communication. I knew it would; she did not.

She delighted in it as I believed she would and then face spelling began. One letter after another followed by a pause. New word, one letter after another and again a pause. This method was used to help her know where a word started and ended. That is how communication began because that's what she was ready for.

Influence caused her to love it. Influence caused her to want more of it. Influence caused her to tell only two people about it instead of the whole world, for a time.

How can you be so incredibly joyful yet afraid at the exact same time – afraid not of me nor communication with me but of the world and its reaction to it? Influence. It is because of the dictator within has control over your thoughts. "I love this, but..., I want to, but I can't, Let's try, Oh, no, not me."

I want all of you to know that those automatic responses need not be.

Positive or negative. I want you to understand that emotional cords are not just negative emotion. The mere fact that you know right from wrong identifies two cords – one that associates to right, and one that associates to wrong. The emotional variances are plenty, but there is a cord that goes one direction or another. The momentary circumstance will lend towards the intensity of the emotion at the other end of that cord.

But the cord need not be a cord. If you get my meaning, cut the cord. Your emotions will soften and, in so doing, life will feel easier because you will have more freedom to choose. Patterns will be broken; new patterns formed. New patterns can be formed based on new information – information rather than influence.

I do not want you to walk around neutral. I want you to walk around informed about your preferences. Then you find out who you really are. You become the whole of you in this lifetime rather than the whole of a million other people.

Be you. But you cannot be you until you know who you are not. You cannot know who you are not until you play with this a little. I want you to play with it – not judge yourself, not dig for information. Be light about this. Have no emotional cord to what you uncover. Just say this word, "Okay," when you find something that has a cord. Okay.

When you find a variety of emotions at the other end of that cord, okay. For some of you that will be enough – awareness. Some of you will find a real passion for this, and you will want to play with it and investigate some things. Do so but keep it light. If you do, true learning will happen for you. You will unleash beliefs. Then you get to find out who you really are. Do you like pizza? You don't know. Do you prefer warm weather? You don't know. Do you like a big house on the lake or condo in the city? You don't know. Do you have allergies? You don't know.

Everything is a manifestation of your dictator within. The one that collects, categorizes, labels and then always disseminates influence. You knew this would be the case when you chose to be a physical human being. You knew there would be influences and you hoped that you would learn to avoid them and find your true preferences.

chapter three

This world that you live in, it's in a different dimension. You decided to come here and have a physical life. You knew that it would contain many different things, including politics, science, history books, schooling, learning, spankings, shoot 'em up bang-bang movies, emotions, homes, money, and commerce.

Mostly you knew that you chose to come here for a reason. You knew what you wanted to receive from this lifetime. So there you have it. Is there a purpose to your life? Yes, there is. We, meaning one among The Teachers and your Guide know what all of the Intentions were for every single one of you – and for every single incarnation that you have ever had – because we communicate with each other.

You, your Soul Being, has conversations with me when you are planning your next life. You also have conversations with many of the entities from the ascended levels. Every life that has been lived by an entity is embodied in within it. It is the entire entity that comprises the Being that rises up to the level of the ascended. But, make no mistake, we don't see the ascended as better. We see them as knowing more and that is why we go to them. We don't feel bad about going to them. They do not look down upon us. We don't carry a cross or burden or baggage of any kind. We are not conceited, nor are they. We are not bold or bashful. We all simply are. If we need something, we know where to go to get it.

We have everything that we need and we share with each other equally, no matter what, because of it. There is none among us that will say you cannot have_____ because you did not learn enough. What we will say is, "I love that you want this. How can I help you? Let's create a pathway for your learning." And then we do.

Some of you say, "Start with the end in mind." I say to you, "Well done." Where is it that you are wanting to go? You say the same thing when you are in this beautiful place that we are in. "I want to become this new thing. I want to do this new thing. I want to engage with these Beings. I want to learn from those Beings. I want to investigate this area of learning." And then you do. There is a purpose behind your decisions.

You always have Guides; you always have Teachers to show you how to do many things. One of the things that you do is communicate with the people in the physical world. You help those that are the maintainers or Guardians of the world. Everything that is in the physical world requires our attention and we provide it happily. It's one of the things that we love to do.

When a tree falls in the woods, we care about it. We take care of it when you chop it up into pieces and throw it on a bonfire. We watch what you do. We want you to investigate why you do what you do and then decide whether to do more of it. How do you know whether to do more of it? Are you helping or are you harming your world, your environment, your physicality?

You, however, are receiving guidance from me in this book so that I can help you decide, so that I can help you undo some of the things that you have done. You being plural, you meaning the world, you meaning humanity in general. I do want more of you to hear us in the mind's eye or verbally, such as that which I'm doing now through this channel. In that way, you have our guidance.

Presume not, because many times you presume things that are not of Source. You presume things that have been taught by way of religion. I love you. I love you through all things. I want you to not kill or maim or destroy. For this reason alone: it causes more like it. It is a chain reaction, only the chain grows in intensity the longer that you or others add to it.

There are other options, there are ways to make and create and do. I know that you look around your world and you say, "But there is not. I need to clear the field. What do I do with the debris? I could haul it away and create mounds, but it's wood and paper or leaves. What is wrong with burning it?"

I want you to understand that there is no admonishment to you for this action. It is but an example of the singular mindset that your world has evolved to. You can create anything. As human beings, you have a mind and you do have ideas, you do have thoughts. Your thoughts are not your own. They are the makings or the product of your environment. They are influence.

Someone who has never seen snow might long to see it, to play in it, to wear the clothes that are necessary. The reason that a person wants to do that is because they have seen pictures or movies, or album covers where snow angels are made.

If you have never done it, and you have seen it, you want to do it. That's what I want for you: to find things you haven't done and then go do them.

Choose things, however, that bring you joy and brings joy to others. Then and only then are you continuing to walk along the path that you set out for yourself. Everything is not connected directly to the Intentions that you placed upon yourself before you came into this life. Rather, it is a hither and yon, a nice meandering, a slow gravitational pull to that which your Higher Self is wanting from you and your life.

When you feel good, intuition soars. You do many things that are of no consequence to you, but they could have sincere consequence to the Higher Self. There might be a person that you needed to meet, just greet them, exchange a glance, and, in doing so, exchange a bond. An exchange of pleasantries to you, but exchange of a bond for the Higher Self.

This may seem meaningless to you, but there are times where there is an

Intention to clear up past aggravations. Whether from this life or another, you know not what can be done to clear things up. You think you need to have direct conversations with the ones that you have had disagreements with. I say no, there are other ways. You call it restitution. This path is not best for you. You can be on a path of harm no one yet harm yourself.

When it comes to the path and Intentions your Higher Self has set for you, the meandering is what takes place. We, your Guide Team, find situations that will be helpful to create, invigorate, or heal bonds that are meaningful to your Higher Self.

You could wash your hands in a clear brook or stream and delight in the cascading of the crystal-clear water. The icy touch feels so amazing. That positive feeling might carry through the day, and because of it you might choose to not participate in an activity or conversation later on. Then, because of that choice, you removed yourself from some other action further down the road. The cascade effect created the opportunity for a simple interaction to occur, for a bond to be intact or strengthened. You do not need to be aware of it.

You may also, because of that happy feeling that you gathered up in that stream, find yourself intuitively guided to someone and a passionate conversation ensues. This is an example of human interaction and not a Soul Intention. That person might come from a different background, and because of this beautiful moment, in which you are in alignment with your Higher Self, you are able to be guided to experience a different kind of opportunity, one of happenstance. You exchange (create) a bond and in the exchange, you are healed from something you didn't know you carried. Again, you do not need to be aware of our guidance in this way. That we tend to you is the point.

I know what is being healed and why. You may never know because there are things that occur while you are having this life that you are not aware of. However, it is an interesting conversation to have with you, to express to you how many different exchanges have had a reverberation effect on your past countenance, meaning your beliefs within.

A simple, yet meaningful exchange might go like this:

"Hello, how are you?

I'm doing well, thank you. Where are you from?

I'm from Ohio. I just stopped in on my way through town.

How do you like it here?

I haven't seen much of it, but it seems rather desolate.

Well, it is that, and peaceful all the same.

I suppose, but what do you all do for fun? I see some buildings but not much in the way of entertainment. We have our families, and we have gatherings with community events. We have folks like you to tell us about the things that happen in the city, and that's a treasure to hear for sure."

The exchange could be just that much, or you might make a fast friend. You might exchange what each of your lives are like and you might enlighten

each other. Or you might just acknowl-
edge that others have different ways of
being and appreciate it or not. You do
not know what your Higher Self receives
by way of your seemingly insignificant,
or happenstance, conversations. They
are synchronistic experiences at times.
You do not need to know when they
are relevant to your Higher Self. I want
you to be happy with each of the
moments of your life.

I want you to appreciate every
experience that you have. I want you
to be secure in the moment, in every
exchange that you have. A fast-paced
life makes that more difficult. Slow and
meandering makes that possible. But
slow is not what this world is about. This

world is about commerce, climbing the ladder, having babies, making your way through life. I want you to live life fully, love life and be happy. When you are, you hear us intuitively and we help you to see kindness, to speak kindness, to look around and appreciate All That Is, rather than receive influence from those around you.

When you are in that mode of being, we guide you easily because the mind is rested. When you are aggravated, the mind is at work. When the mind is at work, it cannot hear us clearly.

When you choose words carefully, you help yourself to undo some of the harshness that is so common in your cultures. Phrases such as, "I would kill to have that, Oh, my God, you're going to die when you hear this, We'll kill two birds with one stone, He makes the most delicious breakfast."

Why do I add that last one? To change the course of your thinking in this moment. You can feel the difference. Some of you will say, "Well, those phrases are meant lightheartedly. We don't mean to actually kill or die." But you have no idea what these words and phrases are doing to your mind. What is done to one is done to a thousand because every thought that's ever been thought remains accessible to the mind, and every thought gravitates to more like itself. Individual "I hate you" expressions can become insurmountable.

I want you to say, "I enjoy this time with you, and I want more of it," instead of, "I love you," because love has been dirtied from of the various ways that it is used. Choose a new synonym. "He captures my attention, He sets my soul on fire" – okay, that last one is not such a good one. The imagery that goes with it is undesirable, to say the least.

Think of it this way: if the phrase you were to use actually came to fruition, would you want it? For example, "They disgust me" – for what is disgust but another word for "I hate, I like you not." There is no specific imagery associated, but the tone is well understood.

You might say, "Oh, you're disgusting," lightly and with a smile, and believe you are being lighthearted. Yes, the tone is different; the word, however, is situated by definition, not by tone. When you say things like, "He makes me sick, I can't stand looking at him, He bothers me so much, He's always picking on me" physical ailments will manifest because you've taught the mind to create them.

You are verbal learners. The world's culture is derelict in its attention to what words can do to the mind and how it will manifest in the body because of it. Choose a softer word, choose a lighter phrase, be someone who pays attention to these things. Shy away from words like horrific. When you use horrific, I still love you just as much as when you choose delightful. But I prefer delightful. When you take a paintbrush to the situation that you just encountered, that paint brush changes. To some degree, so too will the memory that will reside within you about that situation. So paint it pretty, paint it beautiful, paint it well. Words have a lasting effect on everyone.

I want you to concern yourself with you first. The words that your ears hear you say about yourself matter the most. It is how you manifest the world around you, individually. Let's use another example: two people from the same home, same upbringing. One is casual about their references; they join the crowd. The other is more particular and say the words they truly mean. The one that is not so casual or flippant or careless with their phraseology – all things being equal – will manifest fewer physical ailments.

Now, many things go into what the body ingests and then gets repulsed by and produces. Television, commercials, pharmaceuticals, drugstores on every corner, medicine cabinets. The definition itself for that object is just a mirrored door with shelves. It's just a bookshelf in the bathroom, it's a book-shelf, a small one, but it's a bookshelf – or could be. You might not actually use it for medicines and instead fill it up with tiny little self-help affirmation books, and then when you do your business in the bathroom, just choose one. It could be a bookshelf, mirror included. You could choose a book and then look in the mirror and smile about the one that you chose.

But you call it a medicine cabinet. A place where you stockpile all your medicine. Whether you have it stockpiled with medicine or affirmations books or trinkets or money or anything else, you call it a medicine cabinet. When you purchase one those are the words are on your order form, it's on the receipt, your confirmation email. You are ingesting that there is a need for medicine, for you, because of it.

Call it instead my hairbrush pocket cabinet. Call it a secret alcove in the wall. That's a delightful phrase. My cabinet of treasures. Carol is thinking at this moment about what other delightful names could be given to that box in the wall. The mind will get curious about these things when you are free of limitations that the world places on you. Influence can be removed or softened. And when it is, you think differently.

The point being, words matter, phrases matter. What you pay attention to matters. Having a book like this to help you have an awareness is good. Read it cover-to-cover twice and then hand it off to someone else. Play the game where you write your name in the book and the year that you read it, then pass it on until the inside and the outside covers and all the extra pages in between are covered with names and dates. If you get the book back and see that many have read it cover-to-cover and that there's no more room for names and dates, start writing in the margin and continue to pass it on, or buy another just to start a new list.

That is my wish for you, that in a moment where you could say a phrase like medicine cabinet, you remember this little book. You fill up with a little curiosity, a little fun, a little creativity, and choose to think, "How can I say that better? Medicine cabinet is a phrase I can do without. The words in it have meanings that aren't useful or good. How could I phrase it differently? How can I say it better?" When you do, It's fun!

Now, there might be other people in the room that look at you and say, "Why is that fun?" It matters not, because you read this book. You learned from this book. This book is healing as you read it. Hand the book to them next and offer them the choice of reading and healing.

This has been a delight; I do enjoy teaching all of you. This is a moment in time that I have been able to sit here and have a conversation with you in this small book. I like teaching this way, nuggets of wisdom at a time. I like giving you something to hold in your hands that gives guidance from us, that explains things in a casual way, things that you can read and enjoy. Add your own examples and use them. Most importantly, share the ideas with others. Correct them not, but revel in the knowing that you have learned something useful and that you are changing your ways or trying to. Revel when you notice that others are using more feel-good phraseology and that perhaps some do because you have taught it to them.

I love you. There will be more books like this one – some with activities, perhaps, or journals, prompts, and more casual conversations because it is how I like to teach. It is good for you to learn some and then do, to learn and put into practice, and then come back for more. My nuggets of wisdom are for you, for your families, for your children, for your communities, for your world because I like to create a positive influence for you to engage in.

My love for you, is. Period.

engage with The Teachers

GOLD and PLATINUM Membership
Powerful opportunity to engage with The Teachers live with unlimited workshops and/or classes.

Private Readings with The Teachers
With pin-pointed accuracy, they know what you need to know and how to bring clarity to your life. By appointment daily.

Signature Land and Cruise Workshops
Designed as an introduction to The Essential Material and to provide the most powerful teachings on law of attraction and self-healing yet! Each one helps you manifest abundance, on purpose.

Channeled Classes
Live-virtual ongoing weekly classes on how to advance your intuitive abilities, concepts of self-healing and all the ways to do it, and self-paced pre-recorded video courses on special topics aligned to The Four Pillars of Learning that create depth of understanding and overall enrichment of The Essential Material.

praise for The Teachers

When I first heard Carol channel, I immediately thought she sounded like a young Esther Hicks. Powerful teaching every time!

The Teachers validated my mediumship abilities and walked me through what was happening with my own awakening. Thank you. I feel empowered more than ever.

The Grid just makes sense! Law of attraction seemed to be something in the ethers or just feel-good way to think. I am so glad to have found The Teachers and the material they give us. I get it!

Carol, I feel so blessed to have found you. The channeled reading I had with you changed my life. Never before have I felt to empowered!

Attunements are life saving for me! I have no more shy in me, I have a zest for life. I am now strong, healthy, active, and feel so alive!

about the author

Carol Collins is the channel for Jeshua the collective that many refer to as, The Teachers. Her abilities spontaneously manifested in March 2019. After nine months of quiet meditation "face spelling" was introduced as a means of direct communication followed by alpha-state verbal channeling. Through her, they teach about collective consciousness, manifesting with ease, health and wellness through natural healing, and advancing the natural ability to connect and communicate with your Guide – the Four Pillars of Learning that they call The Essential Material. She offers private sessions with The Teachers for readings and attunements daily, signature workshops, and classes frequently. She is a rising star among professional channelers.

To contact her please see her website: americas-medium.com or on all social media platforms as: America's Medium